_____

TO

_____

FROM

_____

DATE

Pearls
of POWER

WORD PUBLISHING
Dallas • London • Vancouver • Melbourne

Pearls of POWER

for Possibility Thinkers

Robert H. Schuller

J. Countryman is a registered trademark of Word Publishing, Inc.

A J. Countryman Book

Compiled and edited by Terri Gibbs

Designed by Koechel Peterson & Associates, Inc.
Minneapolis, Minnesota

ISBN: 08499-1513-9

CONTENTS

Christ within us will help develop our innermost potential for good in such a way that, through the pursuit of our God-given possibilities, we will become the person He wants us to be.

Pearls of POWER

*Every positive
possibility is a trust,
not a treasure.
As a possibility thinker,
I am God's steward,
not the private owner
of opportunities.*

TEN

*P*ossibility thinking focuses
not on the management of time,
money, energy, or persons, but on
the management of ideas.

The human race was designed to be God's family. Then every human being has potential value. Every person has undeveloped possibilities.

There's always somebody
ready to help anybody.

Don't be too proud to tell
people you need help.

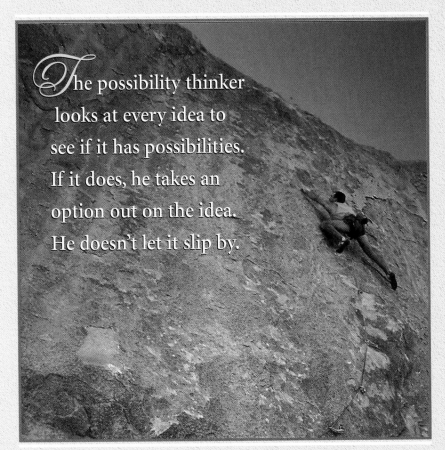

The possibility thinker looks at every idea to see if it has possibilities. If it does, he takes an option out on the idea. He doesn't let it slip by.

FOURTEEN

*Give a little,
you get a little back.
Give a lot,
you get a lot back.
This is the law of
proportionate return.*

The prescription for joyful living
is very simple: If you want to be
happy, treat people right.

Pearls
of POWER

*All it takes is one idea
to solve an impossible problem!*

You won't start winning
without a beginning.

*Don't throw away a suggestion
when you see a problem. Instead,
isolate the negative from the possibility.
Exploit the possibility, and
sublimate the negative.*

Nothing is impossible if I
will hold on to the idea that it might
become possible somehow, some way,
with someone's help.

In the presence
of hope, faith is born.
In the presence of faith,
love becomes a possibility!
In the presence of love,
miracles happen!

TWENTY

We have the power to make any problem better or worse. We do this when we react positively or negatively.

TWENTY-ONE

Money flows to good ideas;
good ideas spawn other good ideas.

Common people are
brilliant if only they believe
in their own ideas.

There are many things
we can't control. . . .
But we can control our ideas
and what we do with them.

SATISFYING SUCCESS

Pearls
of **POWER**

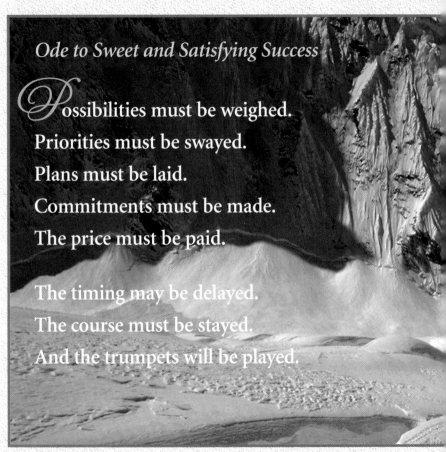

Ode to Sweet and Satisfying Success

Possibilities must be weighed.
Priorities must be swayed.
Plans must be laid.
Commitments must be made.
The price must be paid.

The timing may be delayed.
The course must be stayed.
And the trumpets will be played.

TWENTY-SEVEN

*If our perception of modesty
conflicts with our honesty,
let us tell the truth—
let us praise God for our success
and praise Him for our prosperity!
Then let us enjoy the victory!*

The people who really succeed
are the people who
give extra effort
and push themselves
beyond their normal limits.

The greatest mistake made in timing is impatience. The lesson of patience must be learned loud and clear, again and again, in the process of success.

There is no success
without service,
and service means
involvement in someone
else's wants, needs,
hurts, and desires.

THIRTY-ONE

*G*od can do tremendous
things through the person who
doesn't care who gets the credit.

Possibility+Responsibility=Success

All successful people are
experienced in failure.

There is no crown without a cross.
There is no success without sacrifice.

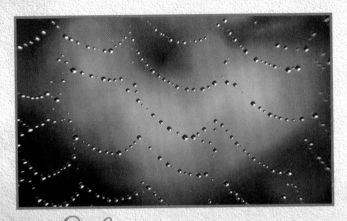

Manage your time, and you'll manage to succeed in accomplishing what appear to be impossible goals.

Pearls of POWER

How do you manage goals? . . .
The answer lies in a simple formula:
Decide—then divide and conquer!

Faith+Focus+Follow-Through=Success

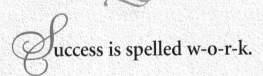

$\mathcal{S}$uccess is spelled w-o-r-k.

Success is not a matter of talent, training, territory as much as it is the skillful and prayerful management of divinely inspired ideas.

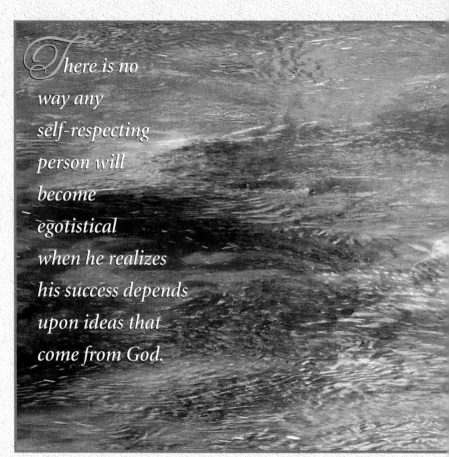

There is no
way any
self-respecting
person will
become
egotistical
when he realizes
his success depends
upon ideas that
come from God.

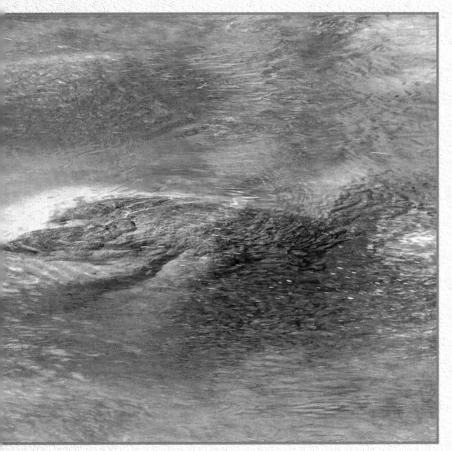

THIRTY-NINE

Success is . . .
the gift of self-esteem
that God gives us as a reward
for our sacrificial service
in building self-esteem
in others.

*Never underestimate the value
of an idea. Every positive idea has
within it the potential for success
if it is managed properly.*

DIVINE DIGNITY

Pearls
of POWER

The dignity of the person . . .
is the irreducible cell of true
CHRISTIANITY.

Read all the self-esteem literature you can, but until you connect with your Creator—God—you're missing the natural, normal connection humans were designed to experience. You need a solid, unshakable foundation for your "I am" and your "I can" spirit.

Pearls of POWER

Human dignity emerges in
redemptive relationships.

*I know the value of my life when
I see the price God paid on the
cross to save my soul.*

Christ, then, is our hope of glory.

In His incarnation,

Christ has honored the human race.

In His crucifixion,

Christ has placed unlimited value

on the human soul.

In His resurrection,

Christ has passed onto the human

race His own glorious ministry.

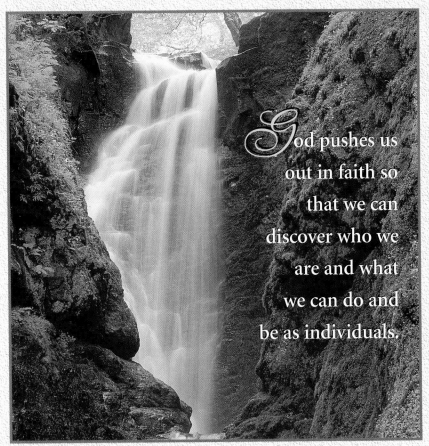

God pushes us out in faith so that we can discover who we are and what we can do and be as individuals.

*The Lordship of Christ is
certain to be a positive
self-dignity-generating experience.
For Christ calls us to trust
His friendship and His fellowship.*

If we follow God's plan as
faithfully as we can, we will feel
good about ourselves.

*Our personal need for divine dignity
is profoundly pervasive.*

No person is too small for God's love, and no service is too insignificant for God's honor.

FIFTY-TWO

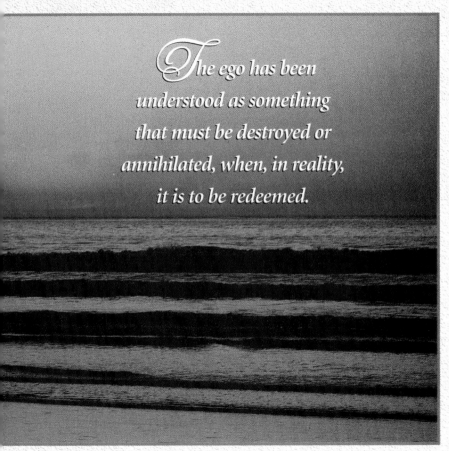

The ego has been
understood as something
that must be destroyed or
annihilated, when, in reality,
it is to be redeemed.

Religion is a sign of health.
Skepticism is a mark of illness.
Unbelief is abnormal; belief is normal.

When God sees a scar. . .
He creates a star.

Let faith be in control of every
decision you make and every
action you take.

SELF-ESTEEM, SELF-RESPECT

Pearls of POWER

The poll makes it clear that
people who view God as a personal,
living, and forgiving Being, and relate to
Him in such a personal way, do develop a
strong sense of self-esteem that is
exceptionally high and healthy!

If we lose our self-esteem,
we will cease to be possibility thinkers.

*Both resentment and
guilt must be washed away
in divine grace before
we can really feel good
about ourselves.*

When hen we are adopted as children of God, the core of our life changes from shame—to self-esteem.

The Christian is on an integrity trip, not an ego trip.

*Trusting persons become
adventuring people,
and adventuring people
discover that when
they take a chance,
together with God,
excitement occurs.*

Only deeply secure people with
a strong, positive self-image dare
to admit that they too need to
grow and change.

*W*hat a brilliant
and balanced solution—
God gives thoughts, not things,
and consequently there is
humility without humiliation,
self-esteem without arrogance.

To build self-esteem in others is to walk in God's will and to do His work.

Achievement in spite of obstacles yields dignity and self-respect.

*The easiest job for God to do
is to keep you and me humble.
God's biggest job is to get us
to believe that we are somebody
and that we really can do something.*

Even as it is the nature
of a seed to sprout,
it is the nature
of love to give
itself away, and
it is the nature
of self-esteem to
treat others with respect.

Everything we do and are will be a reflection of our self-image, positive or negative. Until Christ controls our self-image, He is not in fact Lord over our life.

Pearls
of POWER

*W*hy is this need for self-esteem
so all-consuming . . . so all-important?
It is because we are made in the image of
God! We were spiritually designed
to enjoy the honor that befits a
Prince of Heaven!

CREATIVE CONFIDENCE

*Every achievement is a process,
not an instamatic happening.*

When you can't solve
the problem, manage it.

What we need desperately is the courage to overcome the fear of failure.

Faith isn't a farce. Faith is a
FORCE!

SEVENTY-FOUR

*We should never attack
any problem until we can do it
with a positive plan,
with a creative idea,
with a . . . dream.*

God answers every prayer. . . .
If the request isn't right,
His answer is no.
If the timing isn't right,
His answer is slow.
If you aren't ready—yet—
His answer is grow.
When everything's right and ready,
His answer is go!

If God can inspire me to believe it,
He can help me to achieve it.

*Courage isn't feeling free
from fear; courage is facing
the fear you feel.*

The difference between the people at the top of the ladder and those at . . . the bottom is so basic. The people at the top have learned how to handle good ideas, but those who stay in the middle or at the bottom . . . have never learned to hatch, harbor, and handle creative thoughts.

*C*ourage can only come through
experiences where we run a risk,
take a chance—we win some
and we lose some.

Pearls
of POWER

No person can really love himself unless and until he builds and boosts the self-worth of others.

*I*nsecure people
hibernate.
Lazy people
luxuriate.
Wounded people
commiserate.
Foolish people
procrastinate.
Wise people
dedicate—
they're do-it-now people.

Don't isolate yourself from help, but do insulate yourself from negative forces and negative personalities.

BEGINNING IS HALF DONE!

DARING DREAMS

Pearls of POWER

*Make your thinking
big enough for
God to fit in.*

*Great dreams of great dreamers
are never fulfilled;
they are always transcended.*

*E*very dreamer experiences
a time when things aren't moving,
when progress is bogged down.
I believe that God allows this to happen
to prepare us to receive success
with profound gratitude
and true humility!

You can go anywhere from
where you are—*if* you are willing to
DREAM BIG AND WORK HARD.

Pearls
of POWER

A great goal is like a beautiful old-fashioned wristwatch. The watch is made up of numerous items—springs, gears, hands, dial, and a case that packages the pieces to make a useful and attractive product. Goals too can be broken down into intricate components, which is why goal management is so crucial.

When God gives
us creative ideas, they are
always risky.

Nothing is impossible.
Some things just take longer
than others.

We must constantly pray that God will motivate us to see and seize His honorable goals for our life. Then we must lay a spiritual siege around His glorious possibility to protect it from the temptation to surrender our God-given dreams to the enemy of ease and comfort.

Pearls of POWER

Most people fail to dream because creative desires, daring dreams, and dynamic imaginings are aborted before birth by a subconscious fear of failure.

Pearls of POWER

NINETY-TWO

The most important documents
that shape your future will require
and accept only one signature.
That signature is yours and yours
alone. No proxy is acceptable.
The certificate is titled:
"My dream!"

*ear is the eternal demon
that whispers poison
into the lofty dreamer's mind:
"It won't work. It's not worth it.
YOU'LL FAIL. . . ."

There is a price tag connected to every dream. The higher the honor, the higher the cost.

What bright ideas have passed
through our brain that we've let go as
if we were standing at the railing of
an ocean liner and somebody poured
diamonds into our hands and we watched
them fall through our
fingers into the sea, never
to be caught again?

*The dream
that comes from
God calls us to fulfill
His will by taking
an active part in
His kingdom.*

POSITIVE PERSONALITY

Pearls
of POWER

Don't ever drop the curtain on tomorrow! God's delays aren't God's denials.

Be a positive personality.
Never cause fear and discouragement
to rise in the hearts of others.

Anyone who lacks the ability to deal with delay after delay will fail, fall apart, and come unhinged in this imperfect, complex world. That's why you need to discipline yourself with the positive mental attitude of patience.

Pearls
of POWER

To pursue a problem-free life is to run after an elusive fantasy; it is a waste of mental and physical energies.

ONE HUNDRED THREE

In reality, every problem is only a decision waiting to be made.

Real humility is the capacity to say, "I was wrong; you are right."

If we allow ourselves to live the undisciplined life of a careless disciple, casually allowing negative thoughts entrance, residence, and nourishment in our minds, then we are our own worst enemy.

It's impossible to give without
having it come back to you.

*Love is my deciding to make
your problem my problem.*

*P*ositive pride is that creative
and compassionate confidence
Christ inspired when he said,
"You are the light of the world!"

When we have been redeemed into God's family, we are ready to think big—as God thinks.

A Christ-like spirit of beautiful love comes over our whole personality like an angel of peace when we choose to . . . offer the gift of forgiveness.

*Problems never leave us
the way they found us.*

*You may not have chosen
your tough time, but you can
choose how you will react to it.*

As the birds were created to fly and the fish to swim, human beings were created to breathe the air of trust and exhale the pollution of doubt.

*Only the humble
dare to ask questions.
Arrogance has no time for
the sincere interrogative approach;
it only has time for pronouncements.*

*Loving is he who offers
reassurance to another's hostility,
affection to another's loneliness,
friendship to another's hurt,
and apologies to all.*

*I*f you want to change your world, change yourself. . . . It happens when you meet Jesus Christ and ask Him to take over your life.

*Unexpected sources of help
come from unpredictable quarters
to the person who remains positive
and enthusiastic and cheerful.*

COMMITMENT

Pearls
of POWER

How does God comfort good people when bad things happen to them? He gives them courage, companionship, and compassion. He also gives them a new set of commitments.

Pearls
of POWER

EVERY VALLEY HAS ITS LOW POINT.

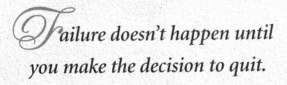

Failure doesn't happen until you make the decision to quit.

*P*eople can block you.

Friends can overprotect you.

Forces may frustrate you.

Enemies may obstruct you.

Families may discourage you.

But only *you* and

you *alone* can defeat yourself.

Pearls
of
POWER

Just, never, never,

NEVER QUIT!

A big achievement
is made up of
little steps.

Pearls
of POWER

*You are your biggest problem
if and when you take your
eyes off of your God-given goal
and close your eyes and ears to
God's call to go for it!*

*Pearls
of POWER*

I can expect obstacles,
barriers, and walls that threaten
to thwart my pursuits, but I believe
God will help me climb the wall
if I'll answer His call.

*B*lessed are the emotionally stable. They have their ups and downs, but they don't allow their down times to distract them from their goals. . . . They hang in there for the entire count.

Pearls
of POWER

More than one person has reached the top because he patiently endured difficult times.

Here is a fundamental rule of life:
If you want people to treat you nicely,

TREAT THEM NICELY.

For every positive action,

there is a positive reaction.

For every negative action,

there is a negative reaction.

Epilogue . . .

So, we are called to join God's kingdom. You and I are called to be modern disciples of Jesus. We are called to think of the possibilities God has for us. . . . Christ was the world's greatest possibility thinker.

DO WE DARE TO FOLLOW HIM?

Pearls of POWER

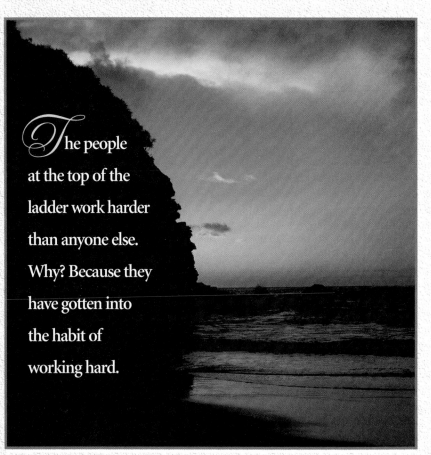

The people at the top of the ladder work harder than anyone else. Why? Because they have gotten into the habit of working hard.

Epilogue . . .

So, we are called to join God's kingdom. You and I are called to be modern disciples of Jesus. We are called to think of the possibilities God has for us. . . . Christ was the world's greatest possibility thinker.

DO WE DARE TO FOLLOW HIM?

Pearls of Power